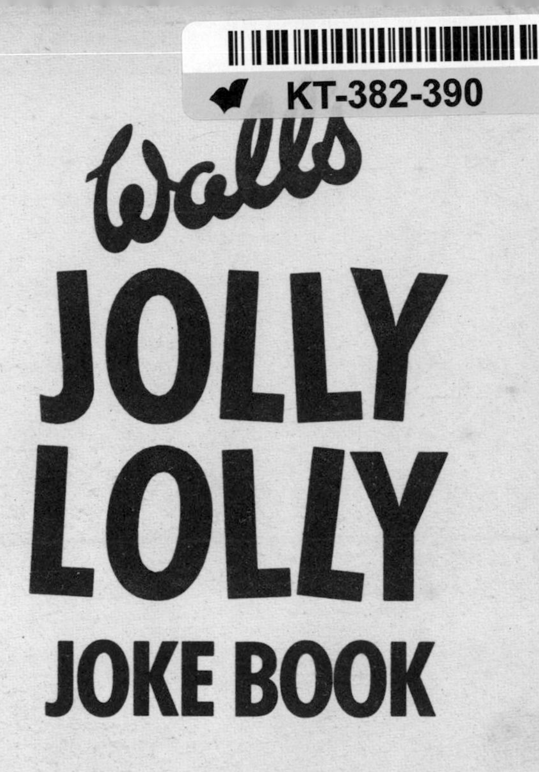
Walls
JOLLY
LOLLY
JOKE BOOK

Other Fun titles available in Armada

The Schoolkids' Joke Book
compiled by Brough Girling

The Holiday Joke Book
Bill Howard

The Grisly Joke Book
David Pugh

Ghostly Gags
Alan Robertson

Graham Marks & Chris Maynard

An Armada Original

To Leo — the inspiration

First published in Armada in 1989

Armada is an imprint of
the Children's Division, part
of the Collins Publishing Group,
8 Grafton Street, London W1X 3LA

Illustrations by Ainslie Macleod
Handlettering by Annie Parkhouse
Typeset by Maggie Spooner Typesetting

Printed and bound in Great Britain by
William Collins Sons & Co. Ltd, Glasgow

How do you make a sugar puff?

Chase it round the garden.

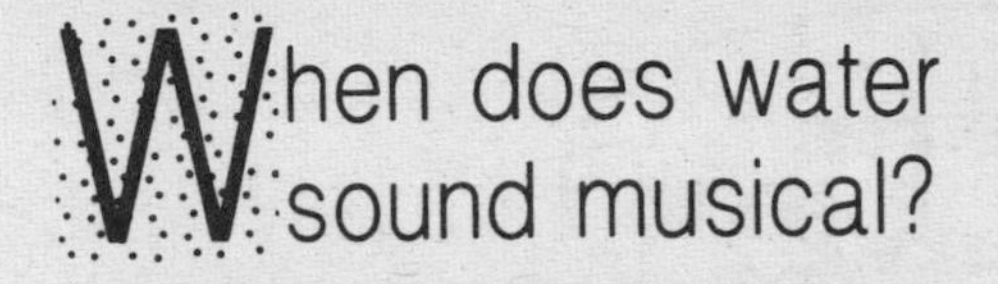

When does water sound musical?

When it's piping hot.

How does Jack Frost travel?

By icicle.

Where do bees wait to be picked up?

At the buzz stop.

What does a bankrupt frog say?

Broak! Broak!

What kind of radio likes to say goodbye?

A long wave radio.

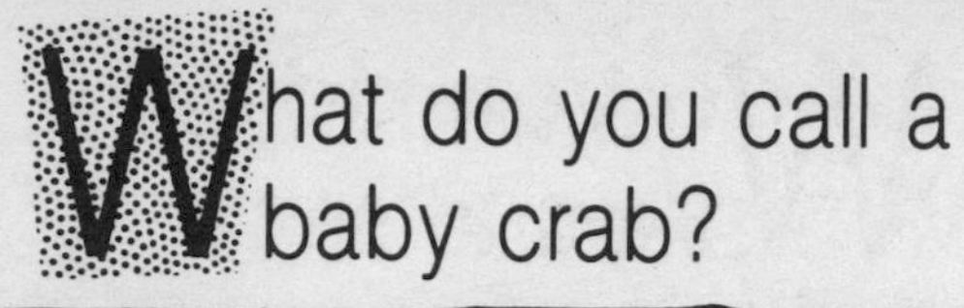

What do you call a baby crab?

A little nipper.

What do you do with a green monster?

Wait until it ripens.

What is red and yellow and cheeps?

An embarrassed canary.

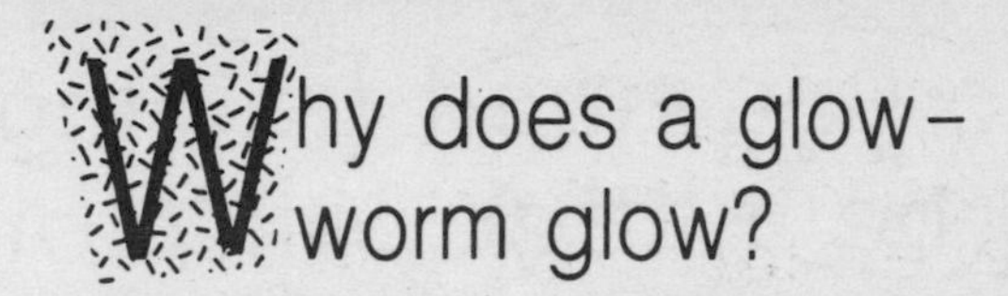

Why does a glow-worm glow?

Because it only eats light meals.

Do you need training to be a litter collector?

No, you pick it up as you go along.

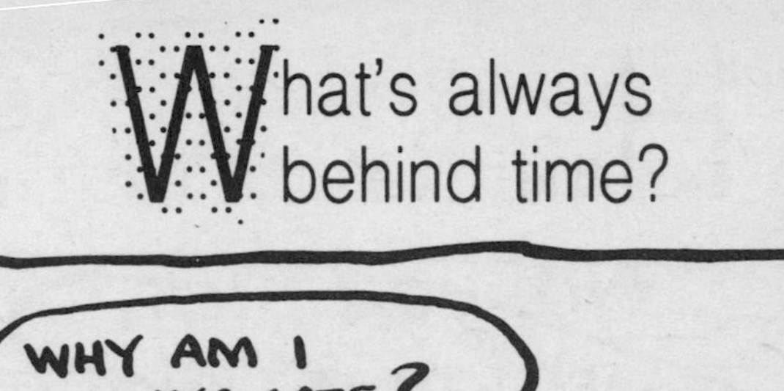

What's always behind time?

The back of a clock.

How do you cut the ocean in two?

With a sea-saw.

Whereabouts was Solomon's temple?

On the side of his head.

What's the best way to get wild duck?

Buy a tame one and annoy it.

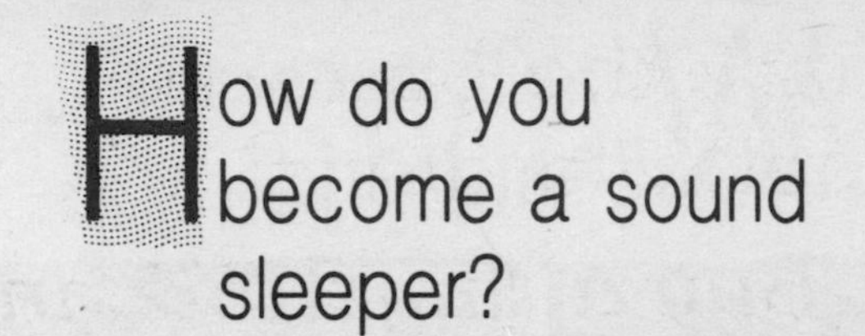

How do you become a sound sleeper?

Take up snoring.

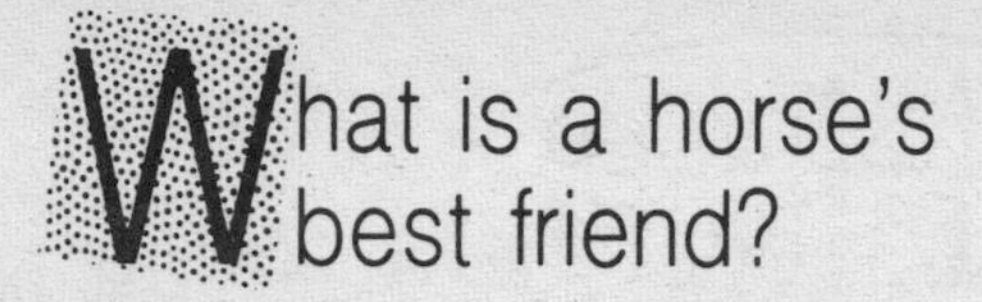

What is a horse's best friend?

His neigh-bour.

How do you get a mouse to fly?

Buy it an airline ticket.

Which is fastest - heat or cold?

Heat. You can catch cold.

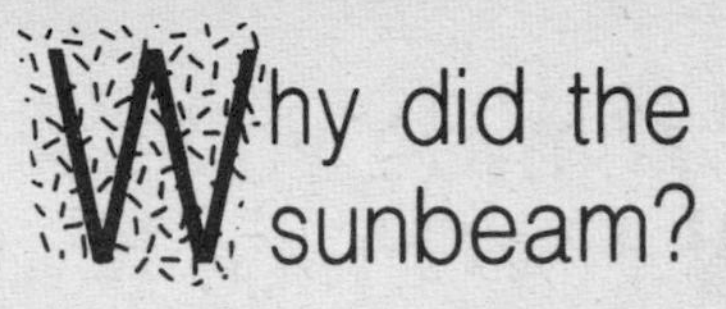

Why did the sunbeam?

Because it saw the skylark.

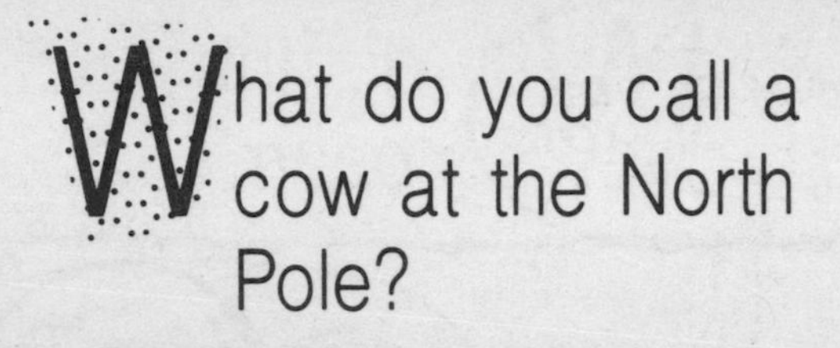

What do you call a cow at the North Pole?

An Eskimoo.

How do you get milk from a cat?

Take its saucer.

What did the violin say to the harp?

Can I string along with you?

What do you get if you cross a cat with a ball of wool?

Mittens.

How did Frankenstein's monster eat his dinner?

He bolted it down.

How do Martians drink tea?

Out of flying saucers.

How do elephants hide in long grass?

They wear green socks.

How do you get in touch with fish?

Drop them a line.

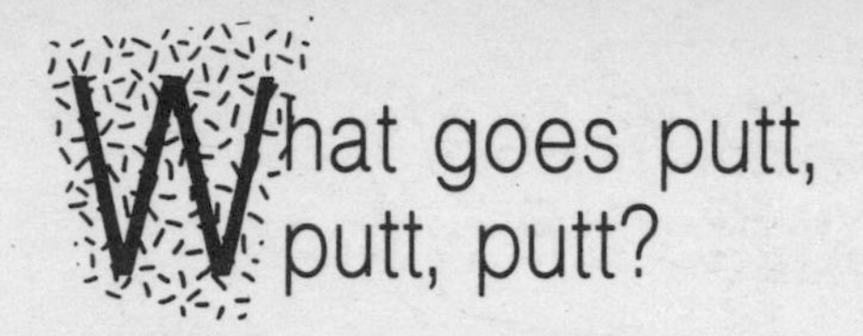

What goes putt, putt, putt?

A bad golfer.

When do mathematicians die?

When their number's up.

Why is an optician like a teacher?

Both of them test pupils.

In what business would you be if you drove your customers away?

The taxi business.

WHAT GIRL'S NAME IS LIKE A LETTER?
KAY.

Why is a heart like a policeman?

Both have a regular beat.

Why did the turkey join a band?

It had a set of drumsticks.

What has 88 black and white teeth and swims in the sea?

A piano tuna.

Why did the bus stop?

Because it saw the zebra crossing.

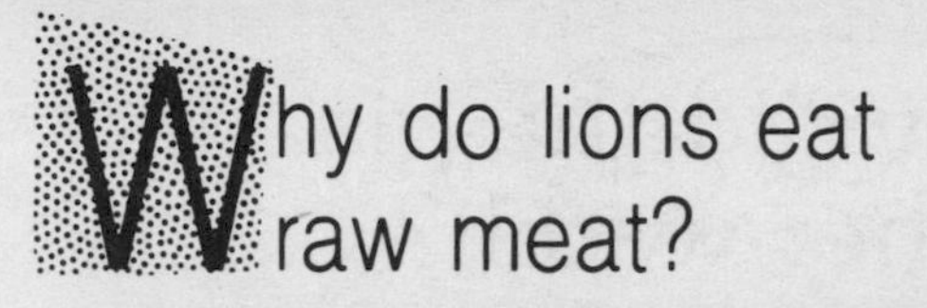

Why do lions eat raw meat?

Because they don't know any recipes for cooking it.

Why did the girl sit on her watch?

She wanted to be on time.

Why don't rabbits have shiny noses?

Because they have a powder puff at the other end.

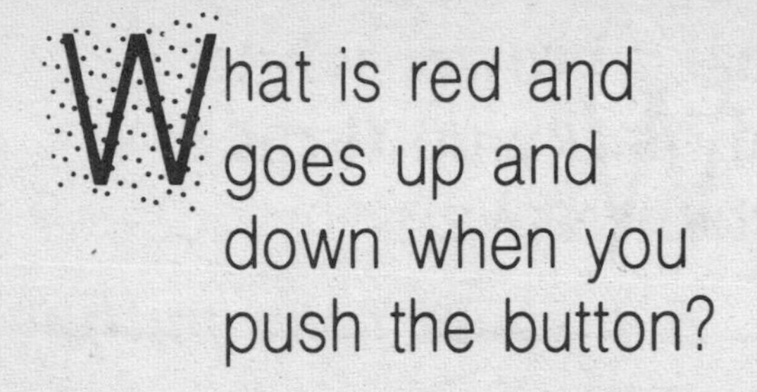

What is red and goes up and down when you push the button?

A tomato in a lift.

What's brown, white and black and turns cartwheels?

A piebald pony pulling a cart.

How do you raise a baby elephant?

With a crane.

Why is it easy to weigh fish?

Because they come with their own scales.

Which animals have to be oiled?

Mice — because they squeak.

Where are British monarchs crowned?

On the head.

Where does a 2,000lb gorilla sleep?

Anywhere it wants to.

How does an elephant climb a ladder?

Very carefully.

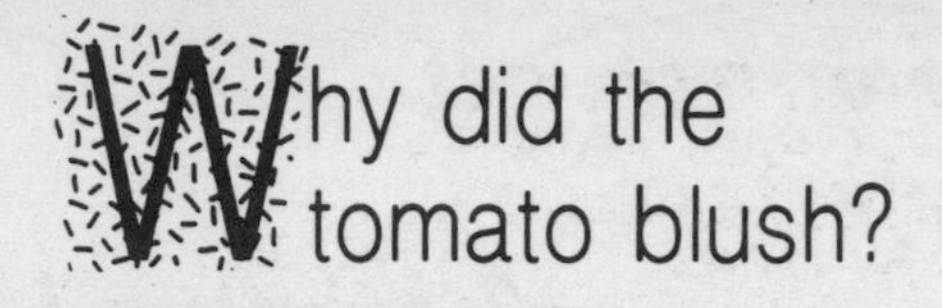

Why did the tomato blush?

It saw the salad dressing.

How do you get freckles?

Sunbathe under a sieve.

When do two fivers make a singer?

When they're a tenor.

Why is a sinking ship like an arrested man?

They both need bailing out.

Does your watch tell the time?

No, you have to look at it.

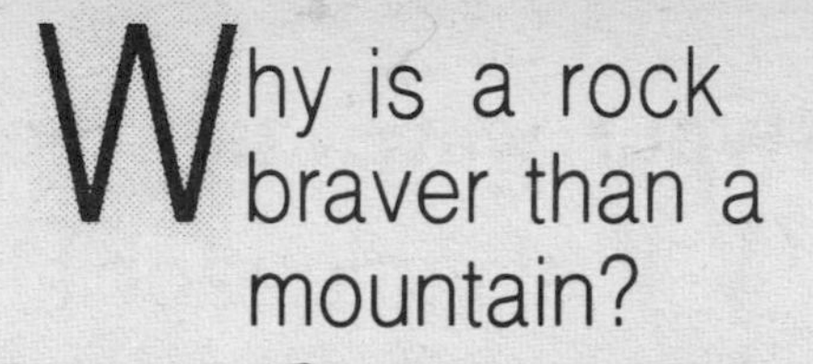

Why is a rock braver than a mountain?

Because it's a little boulder.

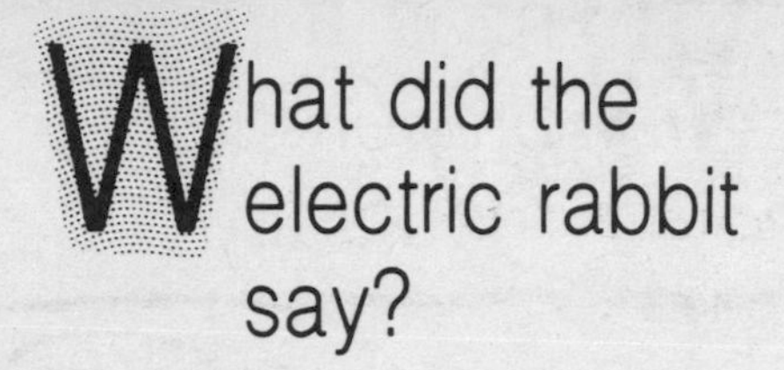

What did the electric rabbit say?

Watts up doc?

What do you call an uneducated ant?

An ignorant.

What stays hot in the fridge?

Mustard.

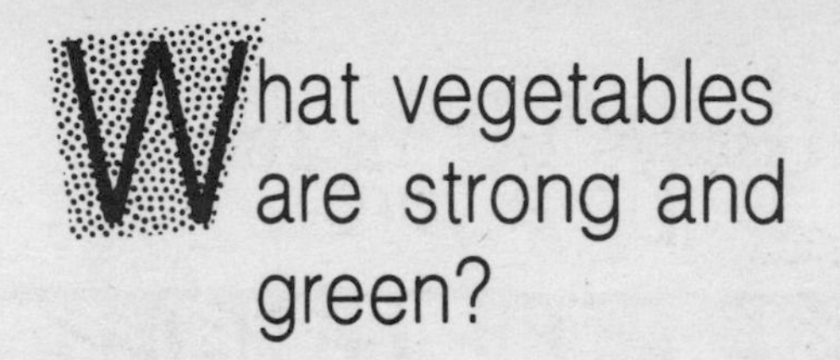

What vegetables are strong and green?

Muscle sprouts.

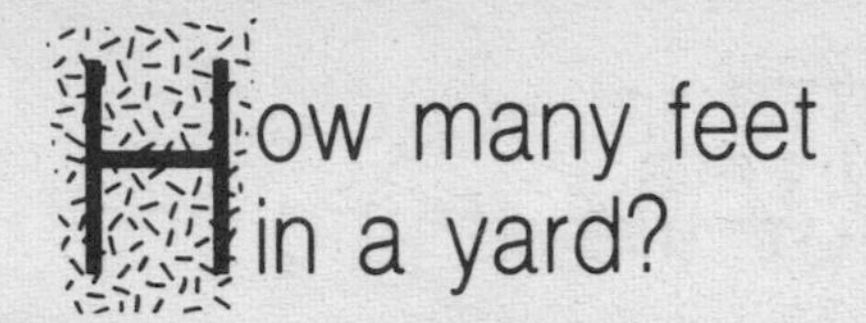

How many feet in a yard?

It all depends on the number of people in it.

WHAT IS A BUTTRESS?
A FEMALE GOAT.

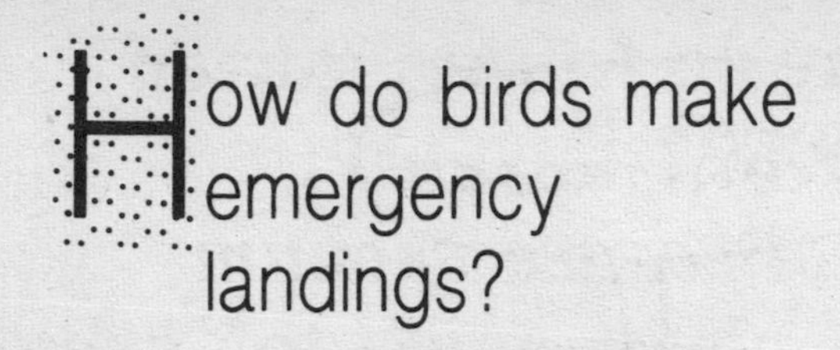

How do birds make emergency landings?

By sparrow chute.

Why do witches ride on brooms?

Because vacuum cleaners are too heavy.

Why are spiders like tops?

They're always spinning.

Which famous detective took bubble baths?

Sherlock Foams.

Why do birds fly south for the winter?

Because it's too far to walk.

How do fishermen talk?

With baited breath.

What is yellow, thick and really dangerous to swim in?

Shark-infested custard.

When should you call a doctor for your fireplace?

When your chimney has the flu.

Why did the maths teacher take a ruler to bed?

He wanted to measure how long he slept.

When are eyes not eyes?

When the wind makes them water.

What do you call a doctor who treats ducks?

A quack.

Which king invented fractions?

Henry the 1/8th.

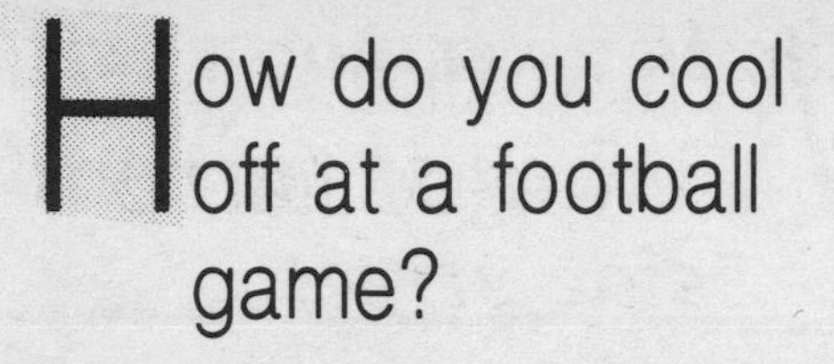

How do you cool off at a football game?

Stand beside a fan.

When is a car not a car?

When it turns into a side street.

What kind of house weighs next to nothing?

A lighthouse.

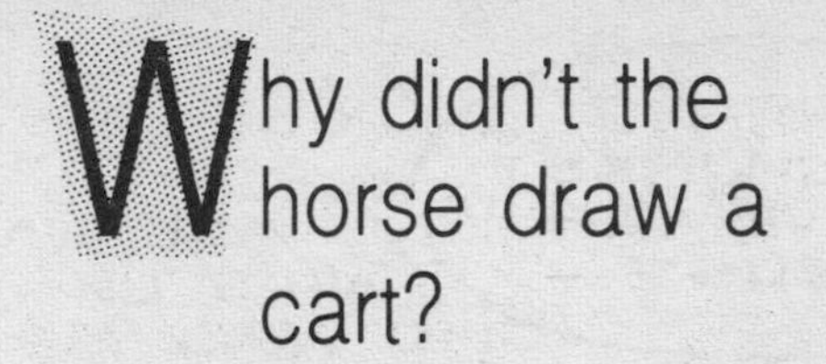

Why didn't the horse draw a cart?

It couldn't hold the pencil.

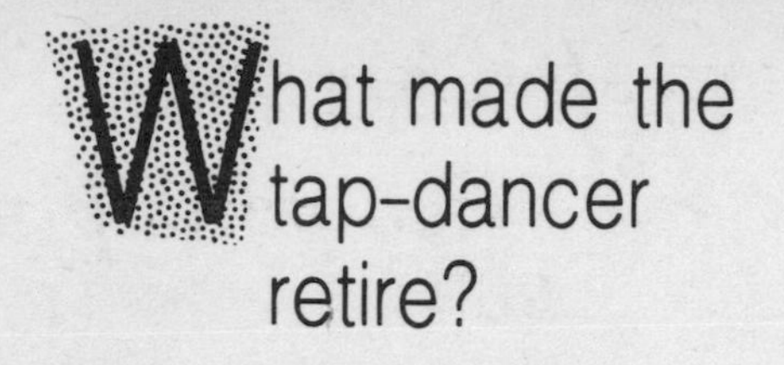

What made the tap-dancer retire?

He kept falling into the sink.

What is a prickly pair?

Two porcupines.

What would happen if pigs could fly?

Bacon would go up.

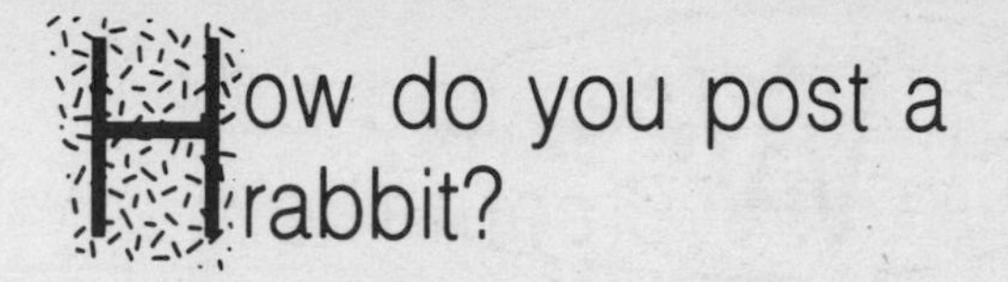

How do you post a rabbit?

By hare-mail.

When is a bad dream like a horse?

When it's a nightmare.

What do baby apes sleep in?

Apricots.

Why are goats so easy to fool?

They'll swallow anything.

What bird is like a gulp?

A swallow.

What runs but can't walk?

Water.

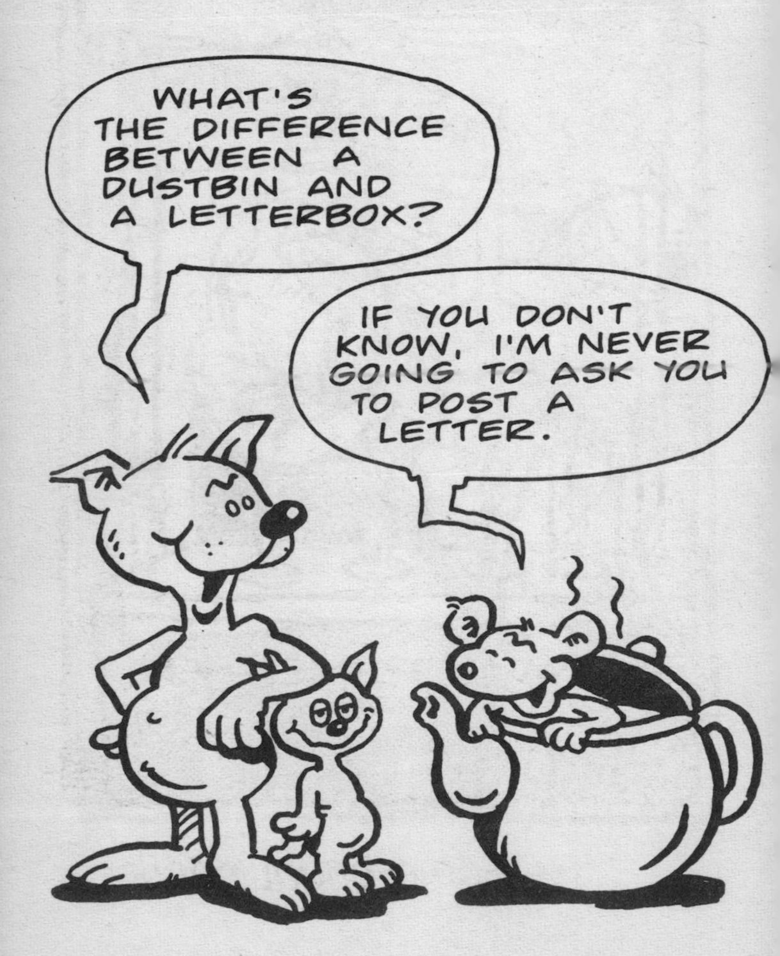

Who invented fire?

Some bright spark.

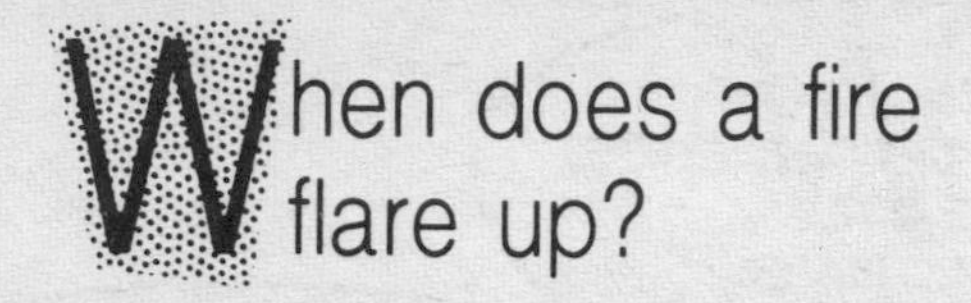

When does a fire flare up?

When it's bellowed at.

How did Vikings keep in touch when they were at sea?

Norse code.

What's the biggest ant of all?

The elephant.

What's a volcano?

A mountain with hiccups.

What lies on the ground 100 feet up?

A centipede on its back.